# TRICKY
## OPTICAL ILLUSION
# PUZZLES

*Jerry Slocum*

*Jack Botermans*

Sterling Publishing Co., Inc.

New York

Compiled by: Jerry Slocum and Jack Botermans
Text and design: Jack Botermans, Breda, The Netherlands
Translation: Machteld Cornelissen, Breda, Carla van Splunteren, Hilversum,
The Netherlands

Illustrations:
Dominique Ampe: pages 11, 23 (*Originals for sale from the author*).
Wico Vos: pages 12, 19, 26 (top and bottom), 52, 55, 57, 63, 70.
Jack Botermans: Other illustrations

Picture puzzles and puzzle cards are from the collection of Jerry Slocum,
Beverly Hills, USA.
© Oskar van Deventer: Matchbox puzzle (page 19).
© Ferdinand/Binary Arts: Laying bricks (page 52).
Interactive Pictures; pages 22, 60. © 1994 Benedikt Taschen Verlag GmbH
Hohenzollernring 53, D-50672 Köln
© for the illustrations of the Interactive Pictures: Fovea GmbH, Bottrop

**Library of Congress Cataloging-in-Publication Data Available**

10  9  8  7  6  5  4  3  2  1

Published in 2001 by Sterling Publishing Co., Inc.
387 Park Avenue South, New York, NY 10016

Originally published in The Netherlands under the title *Optische illusies en andere Puzzels*
by Bookman International bv Heideveldweg 12, 1251 XN LAREN
©1995 Bookman International bv
©Jerry Slocum and Jack Botermans
English translation © 2000 by Bookman International bv, Laren
American edition ©2001

Distributed in Canada by Sterling Publishing
c/o Canadian Manda Group, One Atlantic Avenue, Suite 105
Toronto, Ontario, M6K 3E7, Canada
Distributed in Great Britain and Europe by Chris Lloyd at Orca Book
Services, Stanley House, Fleets Lane Poole, BH15 3AJ, England
Distributed in Australia by Capricorn Link (Australia) Pty Ltd.
P.O. Box 704, Windsor, NSW 2756, Australia

Printed in China
All rights reserved
Sterling ISBN 0-8069-7567-9

# Contents

# Optical Illusions

## Introduction

Seeing is deception! And that is what optical illusions are based on. By this we mean that in general we see things other than they actually are. Our brain often changes the physical image into an image that is more useful to us. Think about perspective and depth, for example. Our own interpretation ensures that our eyes can be deceived. It is not known exactly how it works, but we do know that a tree that is standing appears to be taller than the same tree in a lying position, and that a light-colored object appears to be bigger than the same object in a darker color, and that flat planes appear to have a third dimension, and so on. The optical illusion has fascinated and bewildered people for centuries and, not surprisingly, the list of illusions is both long and varied. Optical illusions can be found in art, architecture, religion, the theatre, in conjuring tricks, and even in armies where grateful use is made of camouflaging colors. Optical illusions were already known in antiquity. Numerous examples can be found in Greek architecture. For example, the Greeks made columns appear taller by allowing them to taper toward the top. And around the year 1000 CE there was an Arabic astronomer, Alhazan, who wrote a dissertation on the "apparent" form of horizon and light. This Alhazan was followed by a long procession of philosophers who attempted to better understand reality by fathoming visual illusion. They fashioned the "images of thought" into basic concepts and principles. History has also seen many artists who have tried to portray in art the image as it is interpreted by our brain. Celebrated figures of the past who concerned themselves with this subject include Filippo Brunelleschi (1377–1446) and Leonardo Da Vinci (1452–1519).

The equestrian portrait of the Englishman Sir John Hawkwood, painted in 1436 in Florence Cathedral by Paulo Uccello (1396–1475), is an illustrious example of optical illusion in art. In his will, John Hawkwood had stated that after his death a statue of himself on horseback should be erected in the cathedral, but the city government were of the opinion that a painting would be sufficient to fulfill his last wish. By working from two different optical angles, viewing horse and rider from eye level and the pedestal from below, the painter gives us the idea that in "reality" we are looking at a statue rather than at a painting. The painted illusion of the statue is known as a "static" optical illusion. In painting, as in this book, this form of illusion appears exclusively, for the simple reason that the flat surface allows no other form of optical illusion. In everyday life, however, we come across other illusions, such as a fata morgana, which is created by "moving" light. The key to the solutions of the optical illusions you see in this book lies in the discovery of a completely new perspective.

Basically, a puzzle picture is also an optical illusion. By making skillful use of our interpretation of what we have in front of our eyes, the creator infallibly manages to hide images. They are concealed in the contour lines of other, more obvious images in the picture. Sometimes, however, the picture must be looked at in a very different way – upside down, for example. It might also be that the concealed image only appears after the picture is wetted, after it is heated, or after it is held up to the light. There are countless other possibilities.
It is not surprising, therefore, that the optical illusion can boast a long history and has been used for many different purposes. For example, in the more prudish

days of the end of the 18th century puzzle pictures, intended for a gentleman's pleasurable diversion, were produced. Erotic images, hidden in playing cards, became visible when the cards were held up against the light. Secret messages were also concealed in innocent-looking pictures. The message could be conjured up by, for example, heating the card or wetting it. Of course, only the receiver knew which method should be used.

The 18th and 19th centuries saw a sudden upsurge in puzzle pictures. Countless cards came on the market, many with hidden advertising slogans. This rage was particularly prevalent in America, France, and Germany.

The puzzle pictures illustrated in this book mostly stem from this period and are limited to visually concealed images – you therefore do not need to heat pages, to wet them, or to hold them up to the light. You discover the solution by looking at the picture in another way.

The fact that the development of these puzzle pictures is not at a standstill is witnessed by the popularity of what are known as three-dimensional puzzle pictures, a few of which are also illustrated in this book. The secret of these intriguing pictures lies in "losing yourself" in the total image; that way, the hidden image appears of its own accord.

Whether you solve an optical illusion, picture puzzle, match, coin, or numerical puzzle from this book, the fascination is always in the unexpected line of approach that you must take in order to solve the problem. A good example of this is the Horse-and-Knight Puzzle. The solution to this problem might appear impossible to you – until you see the puzzle in a whole new perspective, which makes the problem easy.

The fact that the discovery of the solution provides a great deal of satisfaction is illustrated by the popularity these puzzles have always enjoyed. They have continually reappeared throughout the history of the world. Sometimes puzzles attain a magic, even a religious, aspect. Here we are thinking of the mazes and labyrinths which can be found in the floor and wall mosaics in our churches, and of those in the deserts of North America, where Indians laid them out on petrified sandy soil.

Inventing a good puzzle can make you rich, as was proved by Sam Loyd's Buttonhole Puzzle of 1900. It was made for John A. McCall, the president of the New York Life Insurance Co. and designed to help insurance agents sell life insurance. Loyd relates an amusing story. He showed the puzzle to McCall, who was not impressed. Loyd fixed it to McCall's buttonhole and bet him a hundred dollars to one that he wouldn't be able to get it off in half an hour without cutting the string. And indeed, McCall couldn't. Loyd then said, "I'll take it off for you if you agree to take out a ten-thousand dollar policy on your life!" The puzzle became famous and Loyd said it was one of his most successful. The insurance agents must have used it with success: "to buttonhole" became an expression meaning to grab somebody's attention.

*Nicolette Botermans*

# The Missing Numbers

All the numbers in the sum are missing. The only thing known is that
the numbers 1 up to and including 9 can be used only once. Sit down
and figure it out.

# The Sum

$$
\begin{array}{r}
318 \\
303 \\
300 \\
104 \\
+\ 215 \\
\hline
1240
\end{array}
$$

The above sum is correct. Nevertheless, it is possible to delete two of
the figures above the line and still get the same correct answer.

# The Juggler

Cut one of the pieces in two and then make the six pieces into a square.

# Dinosaur Eggs

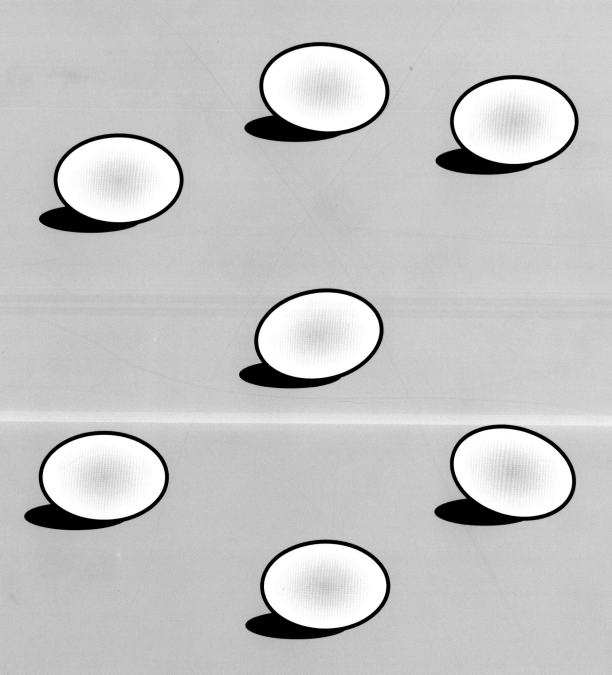

By using three lines divide the page into seven sections,
each containing only one egg.

# The T-puzzle

Copy the pieces on a piece of paper and try to arrange them into a T.
This puzzle first appeared in an advertisement for
White Rose Ceylon Tea from 1903.

# Enamored Pencils

"Really, my Blue, we've known each other now for more than a year.
Don't you think it's time you told me how old you are?"
"Red, my dear, only an eraser would ask a pencil about her age.
But to satisfy your curiosity, I'll give you a clue.
I'm one of a very large family of pencils.
Five years ago I was five times as old as my baby sister, Cobalt.
Today I'm only three times as old as she.
This is all I'm going to tell you. And from the way you take notes,
I figure my secret will remain just that."
How old is Blue?

# Impossible Folding Figures I

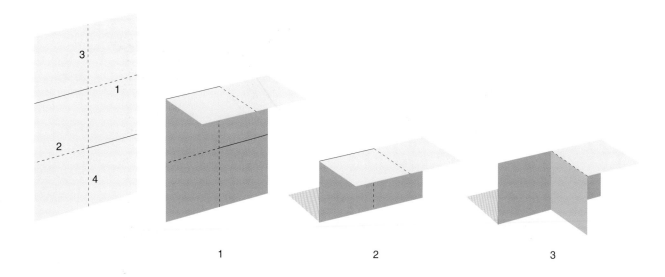

1          2          3

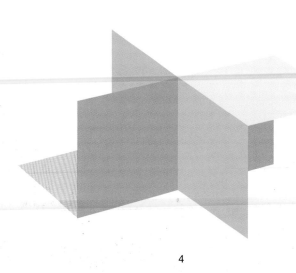

4

Take a three-by-five-inch card and fold it into 6 equal parts.
Cut two of the folding lines as indicated, and fold the card
as is shown in the diagram.
Result...? Quite unbelievable!

# Dovetail Joint

Just another dovetail?
Seems impossible? It isn't. Can you see how to separate the two parts?

# The Mysterious Spots

Do you see red spots in the intersections of the squares?

# Horse Race

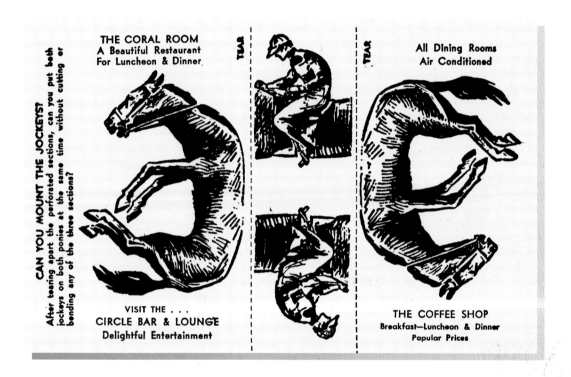

Try to mount the jockeys on their ponies.
Copy the figures on a piece of paper and cut them apart on
the dotted lines.
This puzzle first appeared in an 1890 advertisement.

# Which Gray Square Is Lighter?

Are both the inner squares an equal shade of gray?

# Two Clowns

Which of these two clowns is the larger one?
Use a ruler to check.
This is an optical illusion of German origin from the 1920's.

# Yes, No

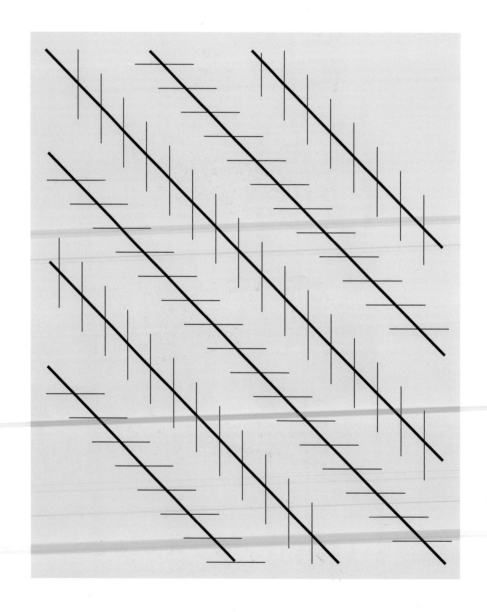

Are the bold lines all running parallel?

# The Matchbox Puzzle

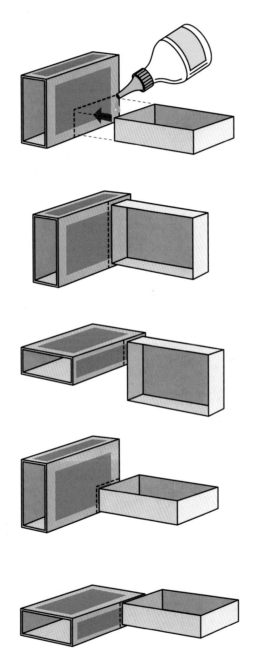

This puzzle is a brainchild of Oskar van Deventer.
Glue the component parts of five empty matchboxes together as shown
in the illustration.
Now arrange them all in such a way that each box ends up in a casing.

# Optical Circles

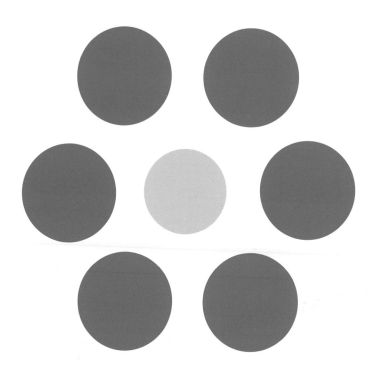

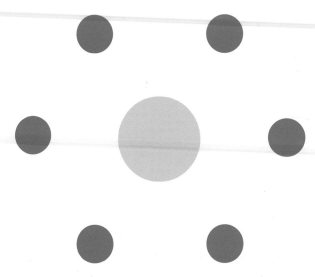

Which of the two yellow circles is larger?

# Fixing A Hole

This handyman wants to repair a hole in the wall. It's 29 inches wide and 118 inches deep. Too bad he only has a 39 x 78-inch piece of wood. How is the board to be sawed so that it can be used to fix the hole?

# 3-D Illusion I

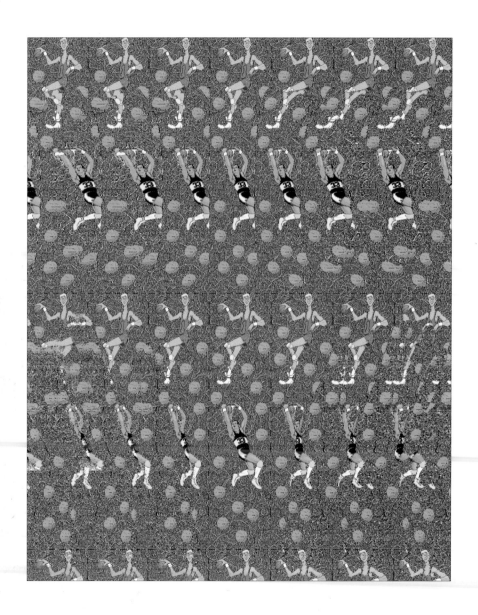

A sporty affair.
Stare into the picture to reveal the ball being caught.

# Twelve Sons

An artist has three children,
two boys and one girl.
He wants twelve boys; he also wants each son to have a sister.
How many daughters would that give him?

# Entomology!

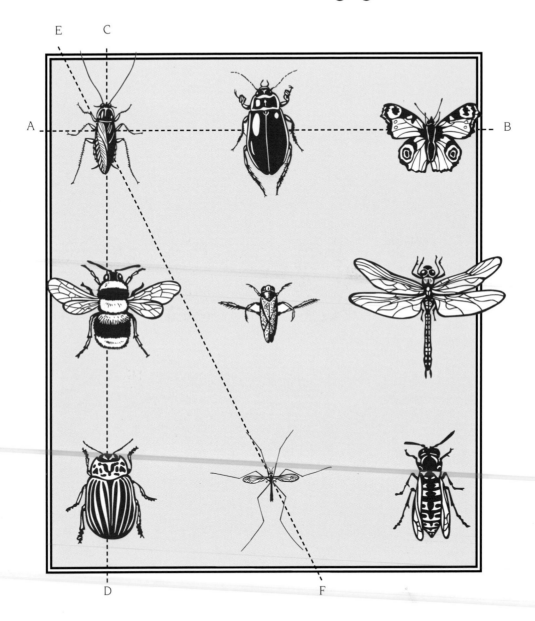

Nine insects have been pinned to this board. In row A-B there are three
insects. The same in row C-D. In row E-F there are two insects.
How many rows are there of three insects, and how many of two?
Remove three insects and arrange the remaining six in three rows of
three insects each.
The life of an entomologist is not an easy one.

# Magic With Numbers

The slip of paper with the four numbers was accidentally ripped in two.
When you add 30 to 25 and square the sum, the outcome is the same as
the total figure on the note!
So 30 + 25 = 55 x 55 = 3025. Amazing, isn't it?
Now the question is: Can you find a different four-digit figure that has
the same magic properties?

# Chessboard Puzzles

The puzzle in the illustration was among other things published in *Sam Loyd's Cyclopedia of Puzzles* in 1914.

Fill the chessboard pattern with the eight pieces. There are three solutions. The same can be done with the twelve other pieces. But then there is only one solution.

# Uprooting The Carrots

Place the carrots in such a way that each carrot touches all the other carrots.

# The Knight's Move

Can you guide your horse in 24 moves around and across this
reduced chessboard?
Each square except for the one you started from is visited only once
and by means of the knight's move, beginning from square 1.

# Sea Battle

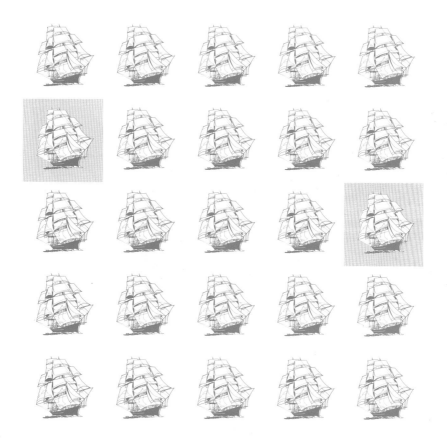

As admiral of your fleet you should be able to connect the jibs of all your ships by eight straight lines without taking your pencil off the paper. Begin and end with the ships in the gray squares.

# Oldsmobile

Find the second car.

# Solitaire

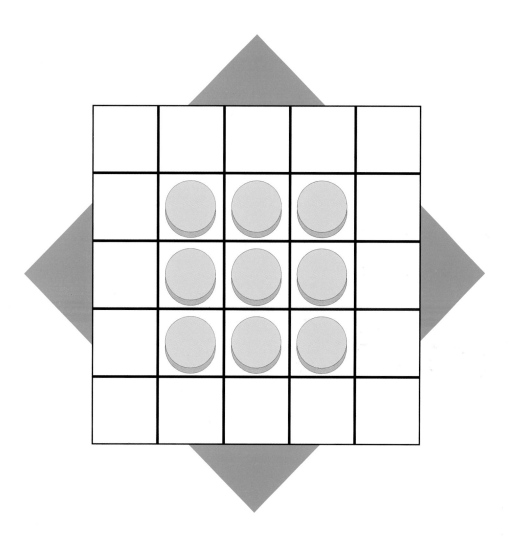

Take any coin and jump another, provided there is an empty square
behind it.
Take away the captured coin. After five jumps one coin should remain in
the center.

# Nailing

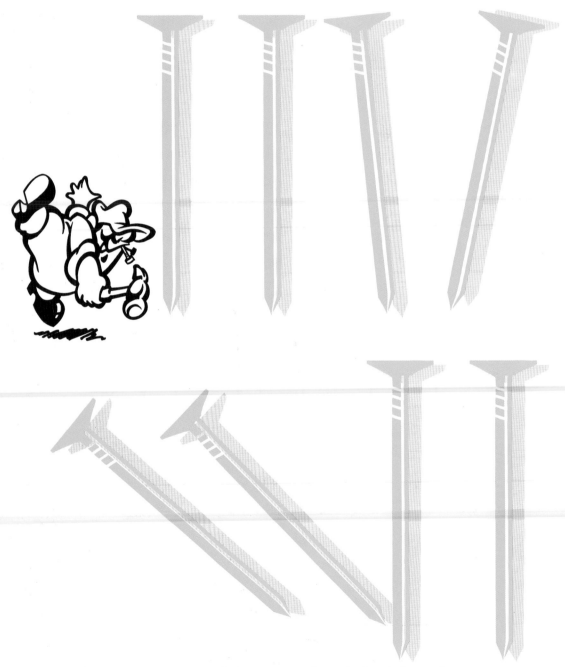

How to balance nine nails on the head of a tenth one.

# Three Squares

Trace the diagram on a piece of paper,
but do it in one continuous line, i.e., without raising your pencil off the
paper or going over the same line more than once.
Now to make it even more difficult, the lines cannot cross each other
anywhere.

# Knots?

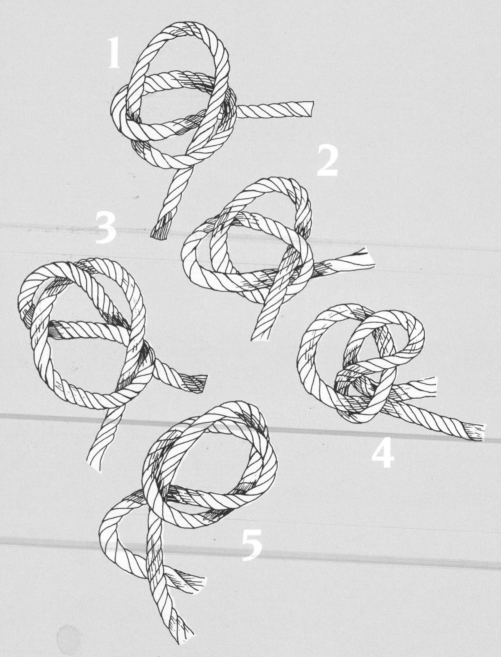

Above you see five knots.
Although they appear to be, they're not all genuine knots.
Can you detect the real ones?

# Tutankhamun

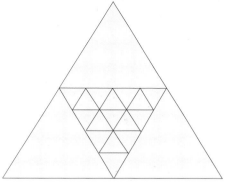

Many scientists have pored over this diagram in the pyramid of King Tut
and wondered how many triangles there were.

# Little Buttercup

Where is little Buttercup?
An advertisement for Malt Bitter (1923).

# Spaghetti Maze

What is the right way to this Italian meal?

# The Smart Bookworm

A hungry bookworm eats itself through 16 books. Each book is 2 inches
thick and the cover is $1/4$ inch thick. The worm starts with page 1 of the
bottom book and ends with the last page of the top book.
How many inches of paper has he devored?
(The principle of this puzzle goes back to 1800.)

# Upside Down

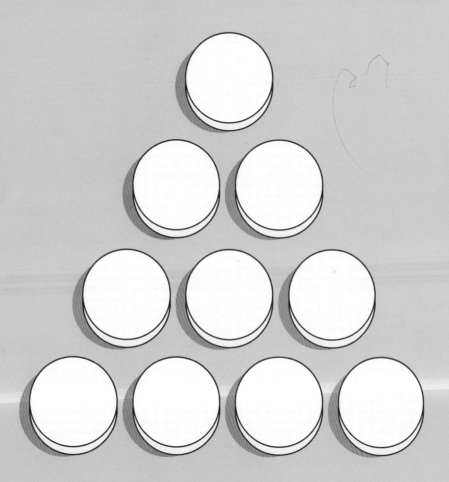

Arrange ten coins in the above form.
By shifting just three coins you can turn the triangle upside down.

# Curved Or Not?

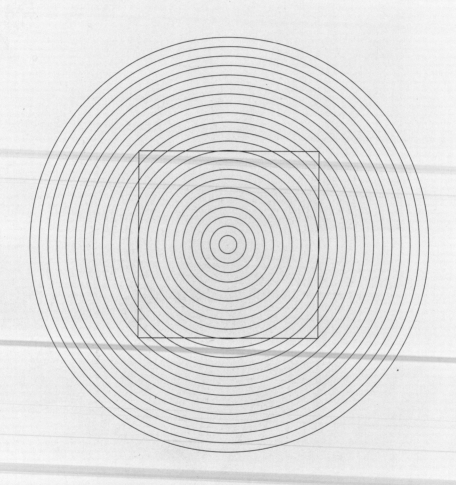

Do the sides of the square curve inward, or not?

# As Proud As A Peacock?

So it seems, but is it true?
Turn the picture upside down!
The illustration was printed on a card from 1880 and was one in a series
of cards known as the American Puzzle Cards.

# Dudeney's Labyrinth

Help the animals find their way back to the woods.
Henry Dudeney (1847–1930) found 600 ways to solve this puzzle without
twice taking the same route or taking a wrong turn at a fork.

# A Piece Of Cheese

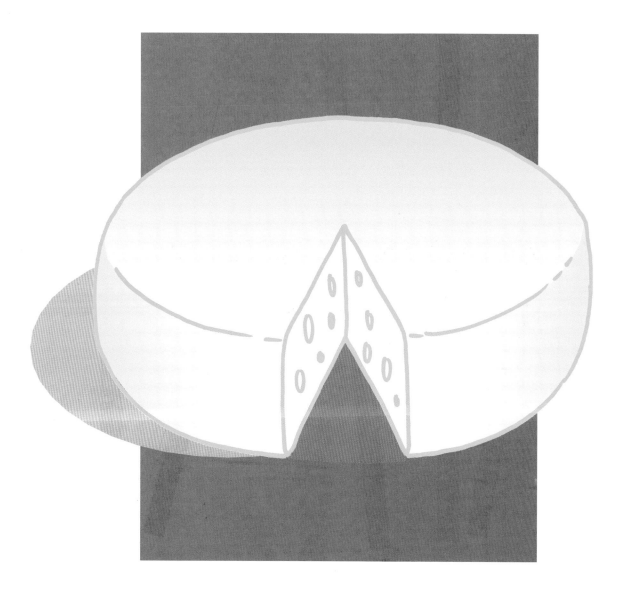

At first glance you would think that someone took a sizable piece out of this cheese. Look again and you will see that it is still there. But where?

# Fortune-telling With Paper

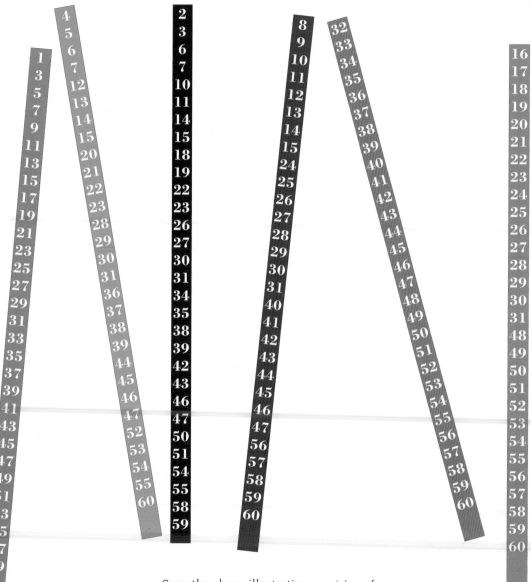

Copy the above illustration on strips of paper.
Find a victim and ask them to think of a number under 60.
Then show them the strips one after another and ask them if the
number they have in mind is on it. If not, put that strip aside. If so,
remember the first number and add this to those of all the strips that
have your victim's number on it.
That will be the number your victim had in mind.

# Cross and Crescent

Sam Loyd published this puzzle early this century.
Turn the crescent moon into a cross.
Use pencil and paper.

# Perfect Squares?

Are these all perfect squares?
No, it is one continuous line.

# Star Material

Twenty of the above pieces cut and folded together make a lovely star.
Perhaps an early idea for Christmas?

# Dangling Pencil

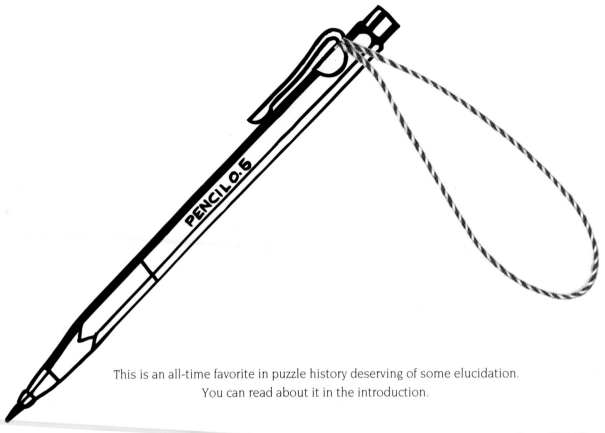

This is an all-time favorite in puzzle history deserving of some elucidation.
You can read about it in the introduction.

It's not how hard the lead is, it's how hard the puzzler
tries and perseveres.
Tie a string to the top end of a pencil. The loop cannot be slipped over
the tip. Attach the pencil to your victim's buttonhole as shown
in the pictures.
Now it's up to this person to detach the pencil from the jacket without
breaking or sharpening it (pretty sharp idea though).

# Belvédère

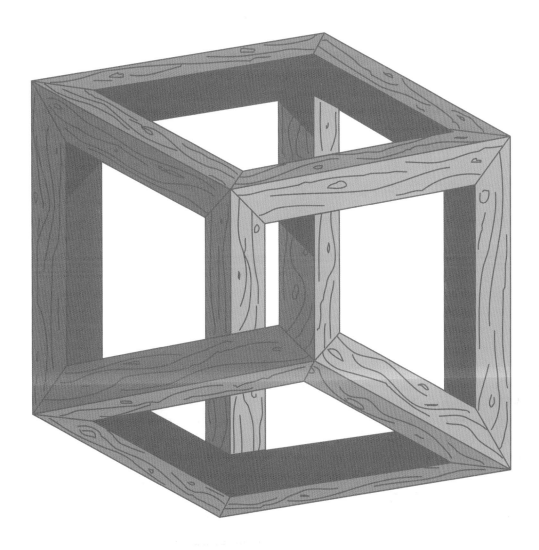

The Belvédère by Escher shows us a man deep in thought
contemplating this figure.
Obviously this figure is quite illusory.

# Just Another Pyramid

Copy the above figures, cut them out, and arrange them in such a way
as to form a pyramid.
Just looking at them, would you say they're all the same size?

# A Little Trick

Happen to have a bill on you?
Take two paper clips and fasten them onto the bill as shown above.
Now, with a short jerk pull both ends of the bill and see what happens.

# Laying Bricks

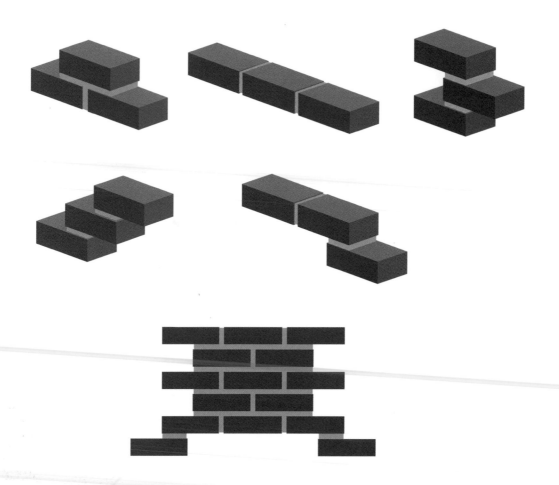

The above wall fell apart in five pieces.
Can you rebuild it with these five pieces?
There is a 3-D version of this puzzle called "Brick by Brick" which was
marketed by Binary Arts Corporation.
The inventor of this puzzle is the Dutchman Ferdinand.

# Pony Express

Map out a route for the Pony Express.
The rider has to collect all the letters in six straight runs.
Use pencil and paper. Draw six straight lines going through all
the letters without taking the pencil off the paper.

# Marriage

Is a man allowed to marry his widow's sister ?

# Impossible Folding Figures II

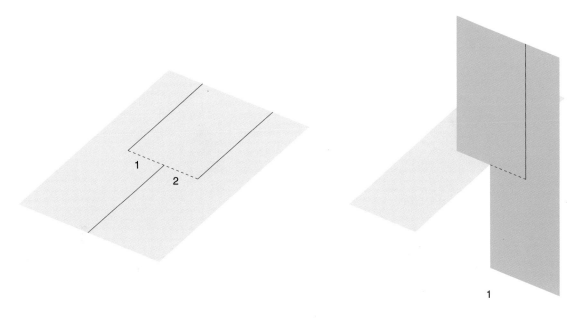

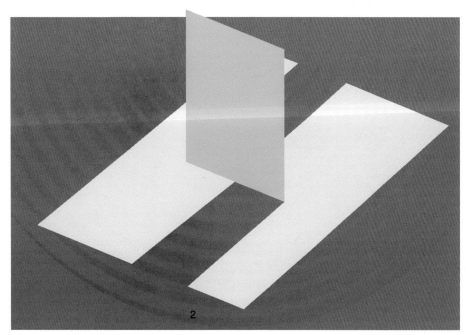

Take a 3 x 5-inch piece of strong paper.
Cut the paper at the three lines indicated and then fold it into an
impossible figure.

# It Looks Like...

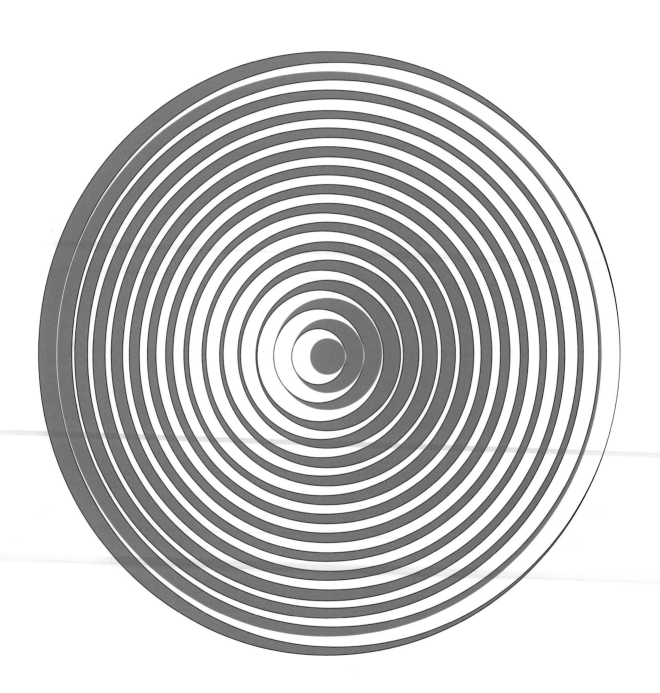

It looks like something is moving - or is it my imagination?

# Never-ending Story

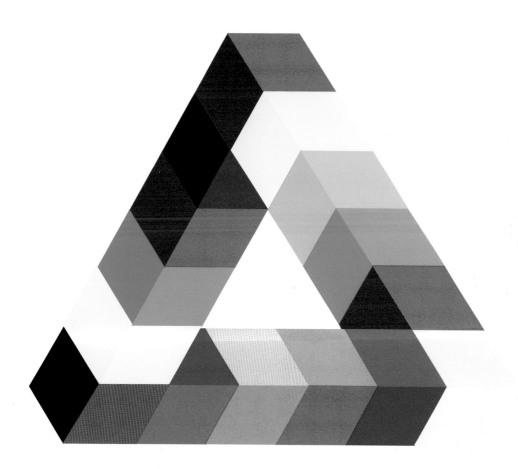

And on and on it goes!

# From Six To Seven

We have here six straight rows of four balls each. Move four balls and
you can make seven rows of four balls each.

#  Betzold's Target

Hold the picture about 6 inches in front of one eye in very bright light.

After a while the black rings will turn brown, the white rings blue, and the central circle bright red!

# 3-D Illusion II

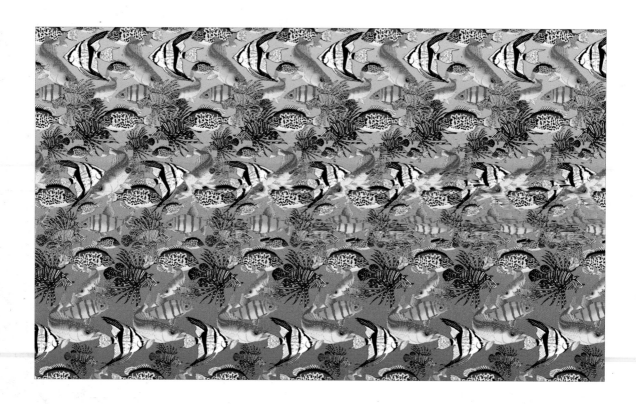

An aquarium full of fish. Peaceful it seems, but danger lurks. Look hard
and see it come to the surface.

# Mason's Disc

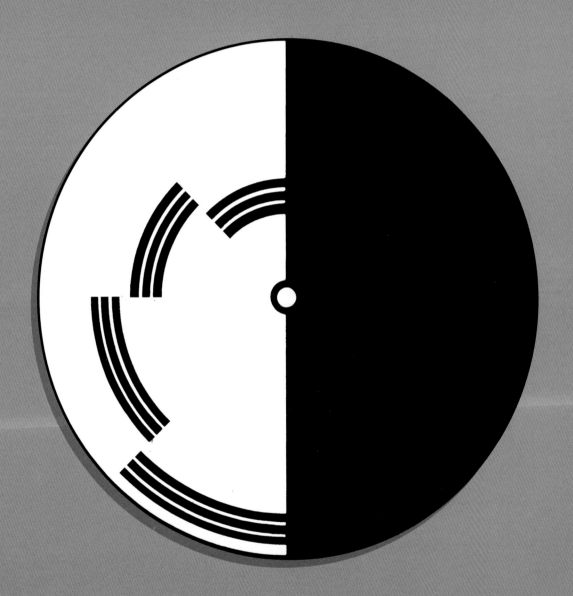

Copy this disc and stick a skewer through the center. Spin the top and
see various colors appear.
The principle of the Mason disc phenomenon has never been proved.

# Presidential Muddle Puzzle

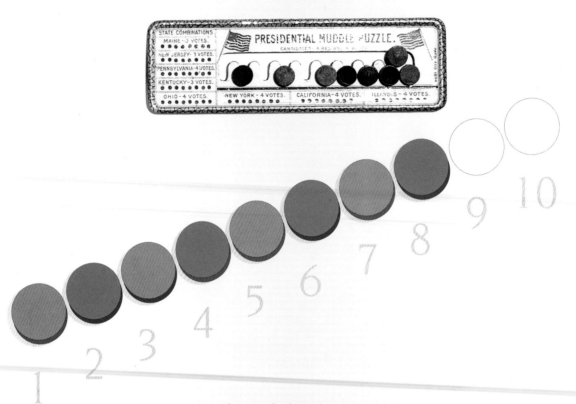

This puzzle dates from 1894.

It comes with an amusing text, part of which reads: *"I am of American construction, the accident of a train conductor and the genius of success. My best friends today are those whom I have earned with hardest effort. Those who love me most are those who study me deepest. I have often wished I could smile at the many helpless endeavors to solve me. The more intimately I discerned the inability of men, women, and children 'to make me out,' the stronger and greater became the proof of their determination not to let me go. I am neither Democrat nor Republican, but I am of the opinion that when both parties get tangled up, as is shown in my several combinations, they ought to be separated."*

For this puzzle use two sets of four suitable like-sized coins, each of a different color. Lay them in random order with two empty spaces on one side. The object is to get one set of four coins on the left and the other set on the right or vice versa and the two empty spaces on one side.

# Impossible Folding Figures III

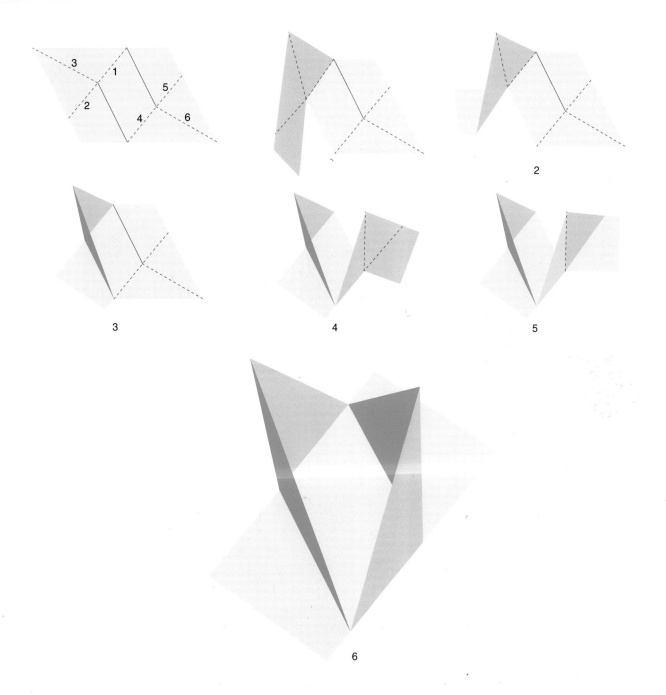

Cut along the solid lines and fold the paper along the dotted lines
following the numbered steps.

# One More or Less

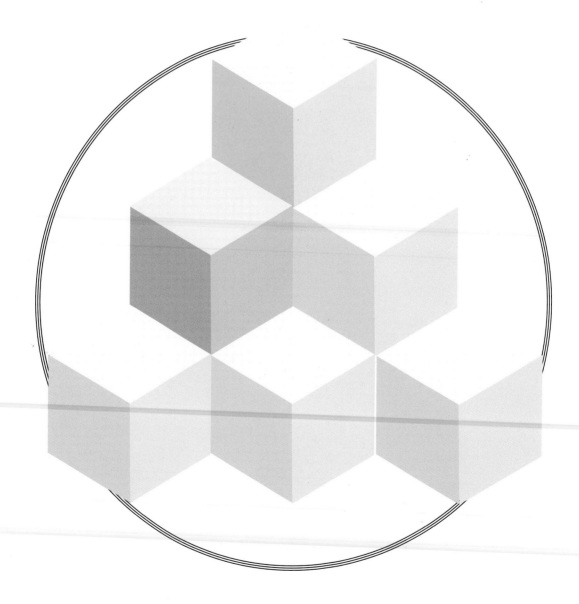

It may seem that there are six cubes stacked on top of each other here,
but look carefully. How many cubes are there really?

# Gone Fishing

A fish's head is $2\frac{1}{2}$ inches long. His tail is as long as his head and half as long as his body. His body is half as long as his total length. How long is this fish?

# Trains

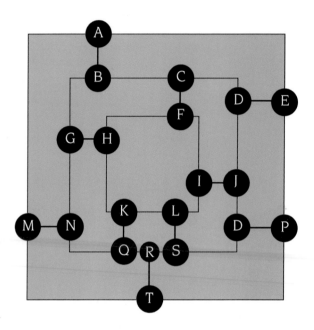

The diagram shows how the train tracks run through all the stops. Now the train has to start in L and stop in each city only once before returning to L. Can you devise an itinerary?

# The Elk

An elk? Or is there more to it? An American postcard from 1911, drawn by C. Levi.

# The Toucan

The toucan has escaped from his cage. Stare at the toucan for a while,
and then at the cage. You will see that the toucan is back in his cage,
but he has turned green.

# Sailing The Seas

Two ships on the horizon. Look at the ship on the left with your right
eye, while closing your left eye. Slowly bring the book closer to your eye
and suddenly the ship on the right will disappear.

# Impossible Folding Figures IV

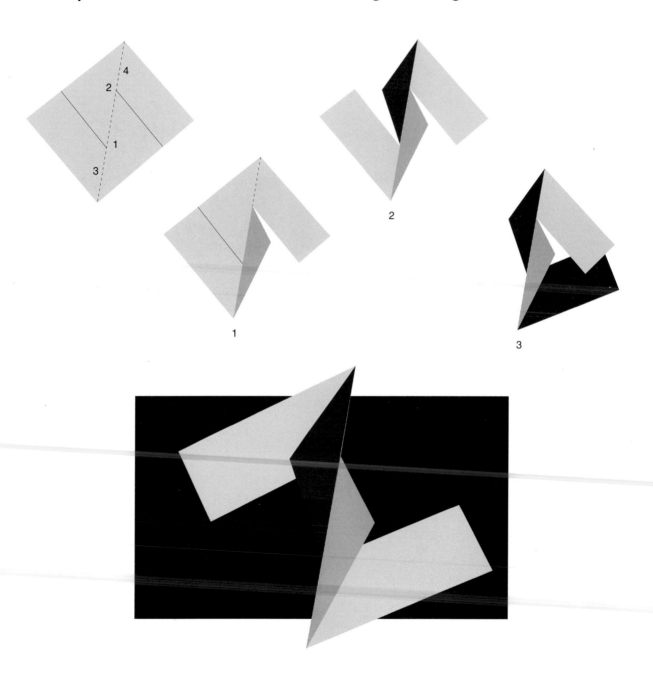

Take a piece of paper of 2 x 3 inches. Cut along the solid lines and then,
following the numbered steps, fold it into an impossible figure.

# Banking

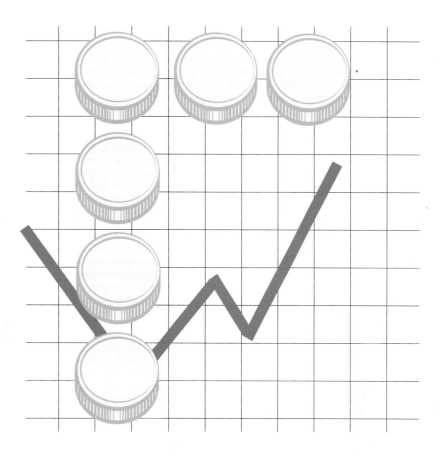

Can you make two straight lines of four coins by moving one coin?

# The Magic Egg

Trace or copy the page. Cut the card along the dotted lines into
three pieces and exchange the two top parts. Suddenly there is an
extra egg!

# Missing Pooch

Puzzle, find the Dog.

Can you bring this lady's pooch back? An English postcard from 1906.
Part of a series called the Valentine Series.

# Cards

**1**          **2**          **3**

a. To the left of the queen there is at least one queen.
b. To the right of the king there is at least one queen.
c. To the left of a heart there is at least one spade.
d. To the right of a spade there is at least one spade.
Which cards are lying here? The image at the top shows the wrapper of
an Indian pack of cards.

# Big, Bigger, Biggest

Which man is the biggest? You'd better measure to be sure!
A card published by Gallaher Unlimited, Belfast & London, from 1913.
These cards were included in packs of cigarettes. Between 1898 and
1939, 94 different series were brought onto the market.

# A La Maison De Paris I

A LA MAISON DE PARIS  1, Rue Ricard, 1
— NIORT —

M. de Crac, en faisant boire son cheval après la
bataille, s'aperçoit qu'il a été coupé en deux....
— Trouver l'autre moitié? —

The rider is wondering where the end of his
horse has disappeared to.

A LA MAISON DE PARIS  1, Rue Ricard, 1
— NIORT —

Il n'est pas de vraie sorcière sans corbeau?

A real witch should have a raven. Where is it hiding?

# Starry Skies

How many squares are there in the circle?

# Equestrian

In which direction are horse and rider riding?
Toward you or away from you?

# The Odometer

The odometer of the car in the picture is at 15,951 miles at the moment when the accident occurs. The irritable lady notices that the figure is reversible. In other words she can read the same number from back to front. Because she is idly waiting anyway, she starts wondering when this will next occur. She decides it will be an awfully long time! But after the car has been fixed, they break down again only two and a half hours later. And again the odometer is stuck at a reversible number. How fast did the car drive in those two and a half hours?

# Salad Days

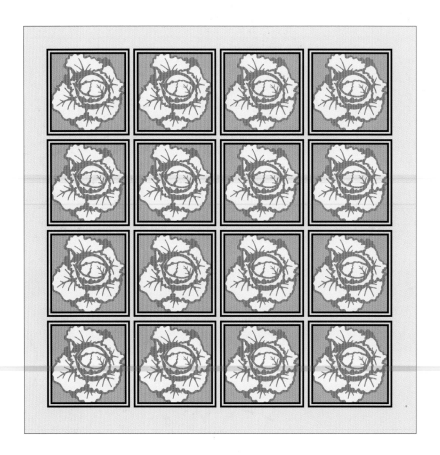

Can you remove six heads of lettuce and still have horizontal, vertical,
and diagonal rows of four crops?

# Find The Presidential Candidate

A card from 1880 from the United States, made by J. H. Hamburger from New York. As the title says, find the presidential candidate!

# Paper Trail

Determine in which sequence these 22 square pieces of paper were laid
on top of each other. All papers are the same size.

# In or Out

Is the spider inside or outside the box?

# A Square Problem

How can the carpenter saw the plate so that he can make a square out
of the pieces? A Sam Loyd puzzle from 1914.

# Dominoes On A Chessboard

You can cover all 64 squares of a chessboard with 32 dominoes. But if
you try to cover the chessboard with 31 dominoes, it will never work.
Which color do the leftover squares always end up being?

# Solitaire

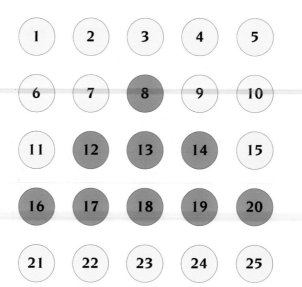

On the blue circles there are coins. If you capture 8 coins the last one should end up in the middle.

# A La Maison De Paris II

The girl is looking for her grandma, to whom she wants to give the laurel wreath.

The elderly man tells tales about the old days, when he danced with Mrs. X. Sadly, she has disappeared. But not entirely - she must have hidden somewhere in the room. Can you see her?

# Magic Square

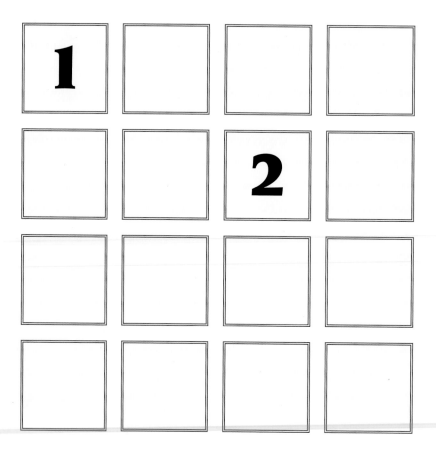

Fill in the remaining squares so that a magic square is formed and you can move from number 1 to 7 with a Knight's chess move.

# Are You Sure Now?

Is the distance between points 1 and 2 bigger than the distance between 2 and 3?

# Line(s)

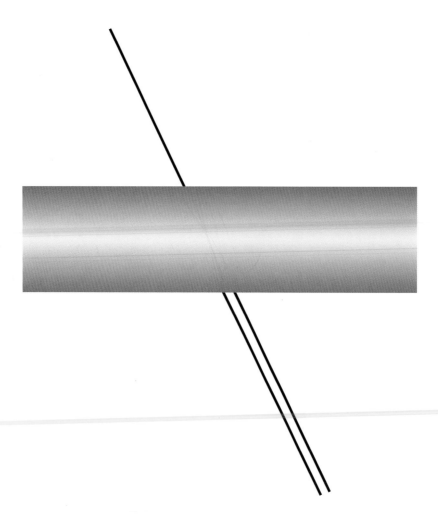

Which line is running under the beam?

## PS

What the next page says is TRUE!

# PS

What the page before says is a LIE!

# Solutions

**P. 6: The Missing Numbers**

17 x 4 = 68 + 25 = 93

**P. 7: The Sum**

**P. 8: The Juggler**

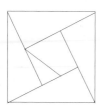

**P. 9: Dinosaur Eggs**

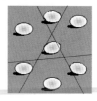

**P. 10: The T-Ppuzzle**

**P. 11: Enamored Pencils**

Blue is 30 years old. Her sister Cobalt is 10.

**P. 13: Dovetail Joint**

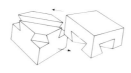

**P. 15: Horse Race**

**P. 16: Which Gray Square Is Lighter?**

They are both equally gray.

**P. 19: The Matchbox Puzzle**

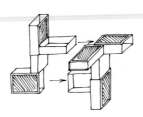

**P. 21: Fixing A Hole**

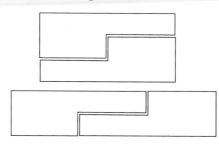

**P. 22: 3-D Illusion I**

**P. 23: Twelve Sons**

One daughter.

**P. 24: Entomology**

There are eight rows of three insects

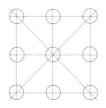

and twelve of two.

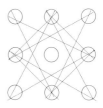

Three rows of three insects looks like this:

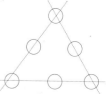

**P. 25: Magic With Numbers**

The number is 9801.

## P. 26: Chessboard Puzzles

## P. 27: Uprooting The Carrots

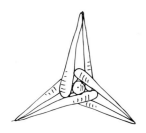

## P. 28: The Knight's Move

| 1 | 14 | 9 | 20 | 3 |
|----|----|----|----|----|
| 24 | 19 | 2 | 15 | 10 |
| 13 | 8 | 25 | 4 | 21 |
| 18 | 23 | 6 | 11 | 16 |
| 7 | 12 | 17 | 22 | 5 |

## P. 29: Sea Battle

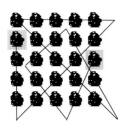

## P. 30: Oldsmobile

## P. 31: Solitaire

A jumps B and C and is recorded as AxBxC. The solution is: ExFx-CxAxG; BxD; IxH; BxI; ExB.

A B C
D E F
G H I

## P. 32: Nailing

Put the nails down as illustrated, then lift them up by using the two nails lying crosswise. Position the whole thing on the head of the tenth upright nail.

## P. 33: Three Squares

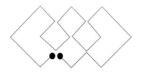

## P. 34: Knots?

Knots 2 and 3 are genuine knots.

## P. 35: Tutankhamun

31 triangles.

## P. 36: Little Buttercup

## P. 37: Spaghetti Maze

Fifth entrance from the top.

## P. 38: The Smart Bookworm

Assume that all the books are lying faceup. The worm eats through the front cover of the bottommost book ($1/4$ inch), then through 14 entire books (25 inches), and finally to the last page of the topmost book (so only through the back cover = $1/4$ inch). That comes to a total of 28 $1/2$ inches.

## P. 39: Upside Down

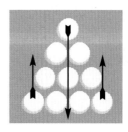

## P. 41: As Proud As A Peacock

## P. 42: Dudeney's Labyrinth

## P. 43: A Piece Of Cheese

The missing piece is sitting upright.

## P. 45: Cross And Crescent

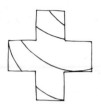

## P. 48: Dangling Pencil

## P. 50: Just Another Pyramid!

## P. 51: A Little Trick

The paper clips will suddenly become linked.

## P. 52: Laying Bricks

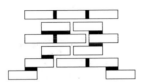

## P. 53: Pony Express

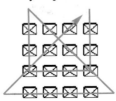

## P. 54: Marriage

It's hard for a dead man to get married.

## P. 58: From Six To Seven

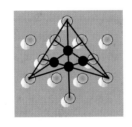

## P. 60: 3-D Illusion II

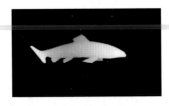

## P. 62: Presidential Muddle Puzzle

2 and 3 to 9 and 10; 5 and 6 to 2 and 3; 8 and 9 to 5 and 6; 1 and 2 to 8 and 9.

## P. 64: One More Or Less

There is another cube standing topsy-turvy in the middle.

## P. 65: Gone Fishing

The fish is 10 inches long.

## P. 66: Trains

L, S, R, T, M, A, E, P, O, J, D, C, B, G, N, Q, K, H, F, I, L.

## P. 67: The Elk

If you look closely you see a courting couple under the elk's antlers.

## P. 71: Banking

Put the coin at the bottom on top of the coin at the top left.

## P. 73: Missing Pooch

## P. 74: Cards

B means card 3 cannot be a king.
A means card 2 cannot be a king.
Therefore card 1 must be a king.
C means card 1 and 2 cannot be hearts.
D means two spades always lie next to each other.
So, card 1 and 2 are spades.

## P. 76: A la maison de Paris I

## P. 77: Starry Skies

Five squares.

## P. 79: The Odometer

16061

The first digit can never have changed in only two and a half hours. So number 1 is your first and therefore last digit in the new odometer reading. The second and therefore fourth digit changes into 6. If the new number in the middle is 0, 1, or 2, the car went 110, 210, or 310 miles in the two and a half hours. So, clearly, it was 110 miles and the car drove at 44 miles per hour.

## P. 80: Salad Days

## P. 81: Find The Presidential Candidate

## P. 82: Paper Trail

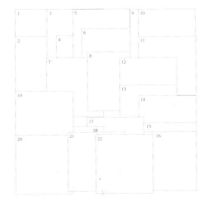

## P. 84: A Square Problem

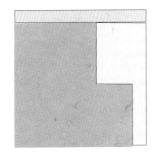

## P. 85: Dominoes On A Chessboard

Two black squares always remain uncovered.

## P. 86: Solitaire

19-9-7, 17-19, 20-18, 13-23, 7-17, 16-18, 25-13.

## P. 87: A la maison de Paris II

## P. 88: Magic Square

| 1 | 8 | 13 | 12 |
|---|---|----|----|
| 16 | 11 | 2 | 5 |
| 3 | 6 | 15 | 10 |
| 14 | 9 | 4 | 7 |

# INDEX